SENSEI NAKAYAMA
In His Own Words

SENSEI NAKAYAMA
IN HIS OWN WORDS

Randall Hassell

LOS ANGELES, CALIFORNIA

DISCLAIMER: Please note that the author and publisher of this book are NOT RESPONSIBLE in any manner whatsoever for any injury that may result from practicing the techniques and/or following the instructions given within. Since the physical activities described herein may be too strenuous in nature for some readers to engage in safely, it is essential that a physician be consulted prior to training.

COPYRIGHT © 2006 BY EMPIRE BOOKS. FIRST PUBLISHED IN 2017 BY EMPIRE BOOKS.

ALL RIGHTS RESERVED. No part of this publication may be reproduced or utilized in any form or by any means, electronic or mechanical, including photocopying, recording, or by any information storage and retrieval system, without prior written permission from Empire Books.

LIBRARY OF CONGRESS CATALOGING-IN-PUBLICATION DATA:
NAMES: Nakayama, Masatoshi, interviewee / Hassell, Randall G., interviewer;
TITLE: Sensei Nakayama - In His Own Words, by Randall Hassell DESCRIPTION: Los Angeles, California; Empire Books, 2017.
IDENTIFIERS: LCCN 2017038511 (print version); LCCN 2017046208 (ebook version); ISBN: 9781933901602 (paperback);
SUBJECTS: LCSH: Nakayama, Masatoshi – Interviews; Karate teachers – Japan -- Interviews.
CLASSIFICATION: LCC GV1113.N35 (ebook); LCC GV1113.N35 A5 2017 (print); DDC 796.815/3092 -- dc23
LC record available at *https://lccn.loc.gov/2017038511*

EMPIRE BOOKS
P.O. BOX 491788, LOS ANGELES, CA 90049

FIRST EDITION 17 16 15 14 13 12 11 10
PRINTED IN THE UNITED STATES OF AMERICA.

ACKNOWLEDGMENTS

THIS BOOK IS THE PRODUCT OF COORDINATED EFFORTS by a large group of selfless people. In particular, thanks are due to Master Yutaka Yaguchi of the Japan Karate Association of Colorado, at whose dojo portions of the interview were conducted; to Mr. Hitoshi Namekata, who provided emergency translation services under the most difficult circumstances; to Bruce Green for his behind-the-scenes efforts; to Tom Openlander for his masterful handling of the photography; to Patty Openlander for the re-scheduling of her honeymoon; to Dave Lowry for his invaluable ideas on the lines of questioning; to Mike Ratteree for making the dream a reality; and to Esther for everything else.

Special thanks are extended to Master Teruyuki Okazaki and the Board of Directors of the Japanese Karate Association, without whose encouragement this book would not even have been a dream.

And of course, the warmest thanks go to Master Masatoshi Nakayama, Chief Instructor of the Japan Karate Association, without whose forbearance nothing at all would have been possible.

FOREWORD

MASATOSHI NAKAYAMA had just returned from his long stay in China when I joined the Takushoku University Karate Club in 1947. At that time, Master Nakayama was assistant to Master Gichin Funakoshi, the founder of Japanese karate-do, and he was Coach of the Takushoku University Karate Team.

After two years of training, I was invited to join the team, and after my third year at the University, all of the team members were required to live in a dormitory provided by the University so we could train together day and night. Master Nakayama would come to the dormitory and live with us two days per week to assist us in our training, and it was during this time that he was living with us that he and I developed a very strong personal bond.

At the end of my junior year, I became Team Captain of the Takushoku University Karate Team, and this added greatly to the personal bond between Master Nakayama and myself.

During team training, Master Funakoshi himself would come and observe our practice once a week. He would sit on the edge of the training floor in a state of deep concentration, and he would offer us his knowledge about techniques and his deep, personal philosophy on the subject of karate-do and life in general. It was at that time that I came to the realization that all of Master Funakoshi's Philosophies, techniques, and ideas had been completely absorbed by Master Nakayama.

There are many excellent people in the martial arts today, but I am convinced that Masatoshi Nakayama is a true master in every sense of the word, and we are very fortunate to have him alive in this day and age to lead us and guide us in the techniques, philosophies, and ways of Master Funakoshi. Master Nakayama is truly a great man.

Master Nakayama's many books, his extensive travels, and his general nature and personality --- being completely open and frank --- have made him a recognized figure world-wide.

I believe that anyone who reads this book and studies the thoughts of Master Nakayama will find cause for examining and re-examining the deeper meanings of karate-do.

Teruyuki Okazaki
Chairman & Chief Instructor

INTERNATIONAL SHOTOKAN KARATE FEDERATION
Philadelphia, Pennsylvania

INTRODUCTION

IT IS NECESSARY TO INTRODUCE MASATOSHI NAKAYAMA only to those who have never been involved in karate training. In the karate world, his name is as familiar as the name of George Washington is to American schoolchildren. So, for those readers who are not martial artists, it is necessary to say that Masatoshi Nakayama is the Grand Master of the Japan Karate Association, the world's largest and most powerful karate organization. A ninth degree black belt, Nakayama is the oldest and most senior active student of Gichin Funakoshi, the man who introduced karate from Okinawa to Japan in 1922. It was under Funakoshi's direct tutelage that Nakayama learned his karate, and it was Funakoshi who officially designated Nakayama to pass the art on to future generations.

It is conceivable that someone, somewhere on earth has not heard the word *karate*, and if such a person could be found, there is little doubt that Mr. Guinness would like to talk to him or her. The following interview is with the man who, more than any other person, is most directly responsible for this worldwide knowledge of karate, the way of the empty hand. It was he who, under the guidance of Gichin Funakoshi, developed and implemented the concept of sport karate in the early 1950's it was he who guided the Japan Karate Association (JKA) from a loose-knit handful of Funakoshi's older students to its present world-wide membership of almost 10 million people in 65 countries and it is he who, although entering his 70s, continuously travels the globe, teaching, lecturing and demonstrating the principles he learned from his Master more than 50 years ago.

To say that Masatoshi Nakayama is a fairly important figure in the history and worldwide development of karate would be in a league with saying that Albert Einstein was a fairly intelligent fellow.

The interview that follows is of historic significance. It is the most complete and comprehensive interview Mr. Nakayama has ever granted to a Western journalist. Undoubtedly, legions of Master Nakayama's followers would be delighted to read an interview in which the Master expounds his thoughts on the technicalities of karate technique, but he made that subject more or less off limits. After all, he pointed out, he has written more than 20 books on the subject of karate, and readers who want his views on technical matters should turn to those sources.

To observe this little man (Nakayama is just over five feet tall) practicing his karate is to observe the human embodiment of the ideals he holds so dear. At the dojo of Yutaka Yaguchi in Denver, Colorado (where portions of this interview took place), 69-year-old Nakayama took off his gi top to show the black belts which muscles they should use in various techniques. One student, a nurse in her early 30s, commented, *"In my nursing experience, I've seen a lot of 70-year-old bodies, but that's the first one I've ever seen that looked like it was 35!"*

Indeed, Masatoshi Nakayama in his street clothes appears to be in his 50's in his gi, blasting young black belts around the room with kicks and punches, he appears ageless.

The highest stage of karate-do, he says, is the transcendence of body and mind-a state in which the mind and body move freely and smoothly, regardless of age or physical condition. Though he would be reluctant to admit it, Nakayama's followers believe that he has reached this state and is moving even farther beyond. *"He's just not like a regular human being,"* one instructor says.

For proof, his followers point out that Nakayama, also a master ski instructor in his capacity as chairman of the Physical Education Department at Takushoku University, was completely crushed by an avalanche while skiing in the Japanese Alps in February of 1971. The doctors gave him up for dead, and his family came to his bedside. There was no possibility, said the doctors, that a man of his age could survive such a catastrophe. Rather than die, however, Nakayama woke up after a few days and announced that he was hungry. Well, okay, conceded the doctors, he might live, but he will never walk again. When he left the hospital four months later and resumed his training at the JKA headquarters dojo, the doctors, like his many students, became astonished believers. *"There is something special about him,"* one doctor said. *"I can only attribute his recovery to his amazingly high fitness level, or perhaps to a miracle."*

But to hear Masatoshi Nakayama tell it, it is no miracle, and he is nothing special: *"Karate-do is attained one step at a time, and so is life. Just train every day and try your best, and the truth will come to you."*

For a man of such enormous accomplishment and power, Nakayama's humility is ingenuous. *"When I get to Heaven,"* he says with a twinkle in his eye, *"I hope Master Funakoshi doesn't beat me up for introducing sport karate."* Then he smiles broadly. *"But I don't think he'll be upset. He wanted me to spread karate-do around the world, and sport karate has certainly done that."*

Masatoshi Nakayama is the living proof of Confucius' dictum: *"The superior man is modest in his speech, but exceeds in his actions."*

The following interview was conducted in part at the dojo of Yutaka Yaguchi, in Denver. Larger portions were conducted in Philadelphia, Pennsylvania, during Master Nakayama's two-month tour of the United States, Mexico, and the Caribbean, under the sponsorship of Master Teruyuki Okazaki and the International Shotokan Karate Federation.

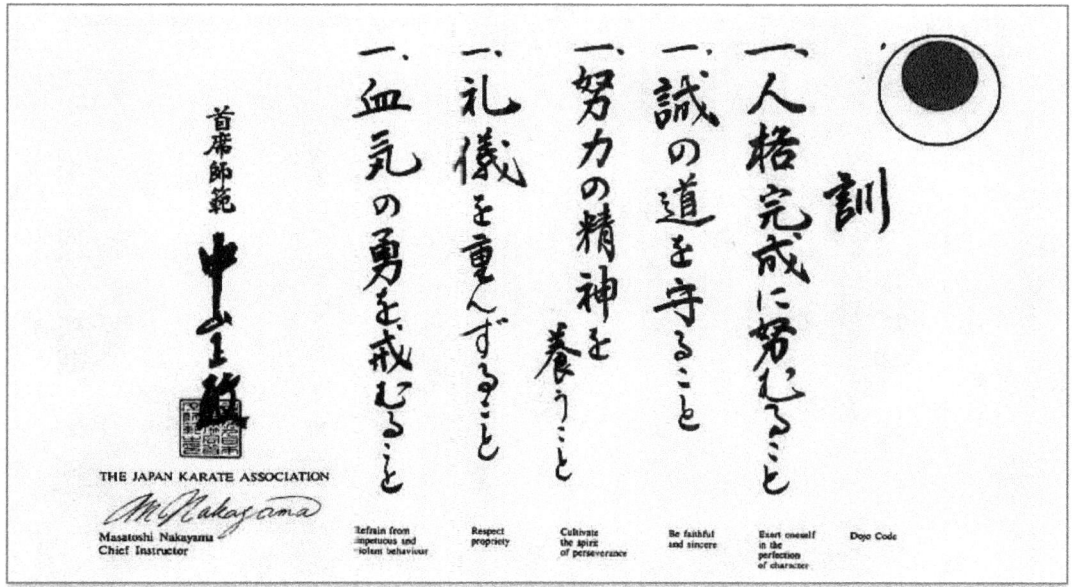

What this interview portrays is the history and philosophy of a man who has devoted his entire life to the cause of karate-do. It is the story, told in his own words, of a man's triumphs and defeats, of his struggles to comprehend, survive, and ultimately lead others.

Masatoshi Nakayama is a living link with the past. He is a living encyclopedia of the art of Shotokan karate-do, and that is where the interview began-in the past where the roots of both the Japanese art and the man had their origins.

When he passed away in April of 1987, due to a stroke, he had set new standards for the art of karate-do and influenced thousands of practitioners worldwide. Master Nakayama was a great teacher in the true budo tradition, and is considered to be among the most influential karate masters of all time. His legacy of excellence, dedication, and true budo makes him an example to all karateka regardless of style, and ensures that the will live on forever in the hearts and minds of those he so deeply and profoundly touched.

MASATOSHI NAKAYAMA

THE SENSEI
In His Own Words

HASSELL: Sensei, perhaps we should begin at the beginning, with your earliest recollection of your life and your family.

NAKAYAMA: My family was for many generations a family of fencing instructors. They were samurai attached to the famous Sanada clan, and they continued teaching fencing up until the time of my father. My grandfather was the last of the line to teach fencing, and my father studied judo. As a young man, he entered the army and eventually became a doctor with the rank of colonel. I was born in 1913 and, because my father was stationed in Taiwan, I spent a large portion of my grammar school days in school in Taipei, Taiwan.

HASSELL: How much did your father influence you in your practice of the martial arts?

NAKAYAMA: I would say that his influence was more of a general than a specific nature. He was what today would be called a strict disciplinarian. In those days, my mother, like other mothers, was largely responsible for the raising of the children, and she did a very good job with me and my younger brothers. But sometimes we would get out of hand, and my father would step in to teach us how to be men. One instance, in particular, sticks in my mind to this day.

As I recall, I was about eight years old and in the first grade in a school in Chiba prefecture. Since I was the oldest, it was my responsibility to look out for my little brother while we were going to and from school. Along the way to the school, there was a large field which was used as a military training ground, and we were forbidden to climb the fence and go into that area. But, like many children, I just couldn't resist the temptation of going across the fence and exploring the field. The field was covered with large holes and craters, and it was very enticing for an eight-year old to explore. So, against direct orders, I took my little brother to explore the field one day. There were all kinds of buildings and army equipment around, and we had a wonderful time exploring all of it. But time got away from us, and it was soon dark. Not only that, but I realized that we were lost. We wandered around that field for hours, trying to find our way out. Not only did we fall into several of the holes in the dark, but the area was populated by raccoons and foxes, and they just scared us to death.

Finally, my father, who was, of course, very worried by this time, sent some soldiers to search for us. By the time we got home around midnight, I knew I was in a lot of trouble. My father told me that I had seriously neglected my manly responsibility of looking out for my brother. This, coupled with the fact that I had deliberately disobeyed, put me in deep trouble. But rather than spanking me and sending me to bed, he told me to stand outside the house until about three o'clock in the morning and meditate on all the trouble I had caused. This happened in the middle of winter, so I stood outside in the cold, humiliated and distraught over the pain and anguish I had caused my parents. This experience had a very profound effect on me, to say the least, and I think of it even today when I am about to do something impulsive.

This can be placed in a little better perspective by considering that when I was born in Tokyo, we still dressed in the traditional kimono and geta. My family was pure samurai, and things were done differently. My mother raised us until it was time for my father to teach us how to be men-samurai men.

HASSELL: Did you study martial arts in your childhood?

NAKAYAMA: Yes, I studied kendo in middle and high school. Some of my grammar school days were spent in Taipei, Taiwan, and in those days I swam every day, played tennis, began skiing, and ran sprints on the track team. I was very athletic. In middle school, I concentrated on skiing and kendo. My kendo training continued right up until I entered Takushoku University, about five years later.

HASSELL: What did you study at Takushoku University?

NAKAYAMA: Well, it was an interesting turn of events that got me to Takushoku University in the first place, and as it turns out, it was very lucky for me, because that is where I first saw karate and met Master Funakoshi.

As I mentioned, my family had been fencing instructors up until the time of my grandfather, Naomichi. Until his time, we had served the Sanada Clan of Ueda, Shinano Province (Nagano Prefecture). But my grandfather moved to Tokyo and became a surgeon. My father, Naotoshi, followed in his father's footsteps and became a surgeon also, and he expected me to follow him into medicine. So, after I graduated from the First Junior High School of Kanazawa, Ishikawa Prefecture, I prepared for the university entrance examinations at Himeji, Hyogo Prefecture. While I was there, the Manchurian Incident occurred, and we were all required to attend lectures on the cultivation of Manchuria and Mongolia, and this stimulated a dream I had always had of visiting those vast and beautiful countries. I wanted so badly to go to China that, against my father's wishes and without his knowledge, I secretly took the entrance examinations for Takushoku University instead of those for medical school.

(EDITOR'S NOTE: Takushoku literally means cultivation and colonization, and it is a university founded in 1900 for the specific purpose of training people for overseas work.)

By the time I was ready to enter the university, I was fairly proficient in kendo, having practiced for more than five years. So, when I arrived at Takushoku University, I immediately checked the schedule to see when the kendo club practiced. But I misinterpreted the schedule, and when I got to the dojo, there were a bunch of men in white uniforms practicing strange, dance-like movements. One of them-a large man over six feet tall-astounded me by repeatedly jumping up and kicking the ceiling with the ball of his foot. He came over to me and told me that they were practicing karate, and if I liked what I saw, I could try it at their next class session. I had read something about karate in the newspapers, but I didn't know much about it, so I decided to sit down and watch for a while.

Very shortly, an old man came into the dojo and began instructing the students. He was extremely friendly and smiled at everyone, but there was no doubt that he was the chief instructor. On that day, I got my first glimpse of Master Funakoshi and karate. I decided that I really liked him and that I would try karate at the next class because, with all my kendo background, it would be easy.

At the next class, two things happened that changed my life: First, I completely forgot about kendo, and second, I found that karate techniques were not at all easy to perform.

From that day to this, I have never lost the sense of challenge inherent in trying to master the techniques of karate-do.

HASSELL: Are any of the people you started training with still active in karate?

NAKAYAMA: Unfortunately, none of the people who started karate training when I did are still active in the art. Most of them have passed on, and that is sad, because I remember always being overshadowed in technique and ability by seniors like Kunio Endo and Koji Matsumoto. But they are all gone now I am the only one left.

HASSELL: What was your training under Master Funakoshi like?

NAKAYAMA: The training sessions under Master Funakoshi were very strict and rigid. During class sessions at the university, Funakoshi Sensei would have us perform technique after technique, hundreds of times each. When he selected a kata for us to practice, we would repeat it at least 50 or 60 times, and this was always followed by intense practice on the makiwara (padded striking post). We would punch the makiwara until our knuckles were bloody. Master Funakoshi himself would join us at the makiwara, and I can vividly remember him striking the makiwara as many as 1,000 times with his elbows. The training was so grueling that of the 60 or so freshmen who enrolled with me in 1932, only six or seven of us made it through the first six months of training. The rest quit.

HASSELL: In those days, did everyone wear a white karate gi (uniform) like we do today?

NAKAYAMA: By that time, yes, but not originally, of course. The gi we wear today was designed by Master Funakoshi after he got to Japan. On Okinawa, the students wore a version of the traditional kimono, but the garment was divided into legs, and this offered more freedom of movement. This garment was called a hakama, and it is still seen in Japan today. But Japan in 1922 was still adhering to a very strict social structure in which different levels of society dressed differently, according to their class.

At the top of the structure were the samurai, followed, in order, by the farmers, the artisans, and the merchants. One of Master Funakoshi's first projects was to design a uniform for karate practice which could be worn by anyone, regardless of class or position in society. After a bit of experimentation and thought, he came up with a uniform which was a combination between the judo gi and the traditional hakama, and it is this uniform that we still wear today. Also, the white color, in addition to symbolizing purity of the intentions of the person wearing it, served to further eradicate any class distinctions among the students.

HASSELL: What would you say is the most significant difference between training today and your training under Master Funakoshi many years ago? How have the technical methods changed over the years?

NAKAYAMA: The technical principles taught in the JKA today are exactly the same as those taught by Master Funakoshi in my day. The methods used to explain and develop these principles have changed, of course. When Master Funakoshi came to Japan, and even when he started teaching my generation, the only training method used was that of kata. The kata were introduced immediately in training, and we practiced them continuously. When we had the basic idea of how the movements were supposed to be performed, we would face each other and make attacks and defenses based on the movements of the kata. Everything was based on the movements of the kata and the application of those movements against actual attacks. This training was very hard and realistic, and I remember many nights when I could not sleep because my arms and wrists were so swollen from hundreds of powerful repetitions of a particular block from a kata.

As I already mentioned, none of my seniors survive today, but they knew only kata; it was the only thing Master Funakoshi taught them. But in my generation, things began to change. The people in my generation were required to study martial arts beginning in grammar school, and continuing all the way through graduation from high school. Karate was not taught in the schools at that time, so all of us had studied judo or kendo. I began kendo training in grammar school, for example, and my friends had also practiced for a long time. But judo and kendo were centered around combat-throwing an opponent or actually striking an opponent with a sword. So, the idea of combat was deeply ingrained in us, and we really needed the combative aspect which karate lacked. Master Funakoshi understood this, and

he began to change his teaching methods to meet the needs of our younger generation. We needed more than just kata all the time, and he realized that things would have to change if he was going to attract young people and see his art grow. So, he picked techniques from the kata and began teaching gohon kumite (five-step sparring) based on individual kata techniques. We would step in five times with the same attack while the defender blocked. Then the defender would counter-attack. But we had high spirits, and if the defender did not counter-attack immediately, we would attack him again, and he would be forced to improvise a defense and try to counter again. These actions became the basis for free-sparring. It was just a natural outgrowth of spirited young people practicing with one another.

Shortly thereafter, we began kihon-ippon kumite, or one-step sparring. In this method, the attacker would announce the target area to be attacked, face or stomach, and would then execute his strongest, most powerful technique.

The defender had only one chance to make a powerful, correct block and counter-attack. This was very much in keeping with the basic philosophy of martial art, which revolves around the concept that there is no second chance. Everything must be done correctly the first time, or the person dies. We weren't trying to kill each other, of course, but we were trying to execute that one, perfect technique that would stop the opponent in a real fighting situation.

A natural outgrowth of this kind of training was jyu-ippon kumite (one-step sparring), in which the defender knew the area to be attacked, but in which the attacker could maneuver freely for position and distancing.

The significant thing about this is that this was the first time karate had been taught in any way except for application of kata movements to self-defense, and the entire system of kumite (sparring) developed in a single, five-year period. When Master Funakoshi published Karate-do Kyohan (The Master Text of Karate-do) in 1936, he included basic sparring methods in the book, and this was the first time this brand-new idea was introduced to the public at large.

Also in this period came the idea of practicing each technique by itself, as we do today. Master Funakoshi felt that we should practice each technique independently to develop the feeling of "ikken hisatsu" (to stop the opponent with one blow) in our sparring. So we started practicing each technique by itself, marching up and down the floor, repeating the technique again and again. This is today the fundamental method of basic training.

During my first five years in college, karate training was divided into the three main aspects we know today—kihon (basic training), kata, and kumite.

I began training in 1932, and basic kumite was introduced in 1933. In 1934, jyu-ippon kumite was introduced, and jyu kumite (free sparring) began in 1935. In November of 1936, we formed the All Japan Collegiate Karate Union and gave a demonstration at the Tokyo Civic Center. For the first time in history, we showed the public the new training methods of kumite, and demonstrated how the student progresses from five-step sparring to one-step, then to semi-free and finally free sparring.

At that time, we didn't have a karate dojo. Master Funakoshi was teaching in colleges, and he was teaching private groups from companies and the Tokyo Bar Association. A number of us, however, wanted more training than was available in college, so we would get together in the evenings and go to Master Funakoshi's house for more training at night.

At the university, we would train for two hours at noon, and then we would go to Master Funakoshi's house in the evening for three more hours of training. At his house, Master Funakoshi had a wooden deck' which was really just a stairway with a little porch. While we trained, Master Funakoshi and his son, Yoshitaka, would sit on the floor on one end of the area and teach us. This was a very old method of teaching, and it was believed that the sensei could more fully concentrate on the movements of the students by sitting still and concentrating deeply. From time to time, Master Funakoshi would stand up and demonstrate a technique or explain a particular point, and then sit down again. I remember him sitting there with his back very straight and rigid, and often he would remain in that position for a full three hours, moving only when he wanted to show us some detail.

The deck at Master Funakoshi's house was so small that only a couple of us could practice at one time, and since we often trained until after dark, we would frequently bump into one another. Of course, at this time, Master Funakoshi was not at all a wealthy man, so all of the students pooled our money and donated it to Master Funakoshi so he could expand his stairway, and this helped a great deal.

HASSELL: It is well known that Master Funakoshi wrote the first book on karate-do, "Karate-do Kyohan," and that he changed the characters for karate from the older meaning of Chinese hand to empty hand. How were these actions received by karate people and the general public?

NAKAYAMA: Well, the characters for karate had become rather well known by the 1930s, but they were still read "Chinese hand." In 1935, Master Funakoshi wrote "Karate-do Kyohan" and proposed that the characters be changed to "empty hand" to more accurately reflect the nature of karate as a Japanese art. But more importantly, he also proposed that karate-jutsu, the technique of karate, be changed to karate-do, karate as a way of life. This caused a

tremendous uproar among some of the older, more traditional Okinawan karate masters of the time, and they took a strong stand against him in the newspapers. They demanded to know why he wanted to remove karate from its Okinawan and Chinese roots. His reply to them was very interesting. He said, in effect, that since karate had spread to the Japanese mainland and been accepted by the intelligentsia in Japan, it had ceased to be a local, Okinawan martial art. He said it had grown to universal proportions and acceptance, and should therefore be elevated to equal status with kendo, Japan's oldest martial art, and judo, which was very popular. The character he chose for kara is from the Buddhist tradition and is also pronounced "ku," which means "void" or "empty" and signifies the universe.

For two years, letters and articles flew back and forth between Master Funakoshi and the Okinawans in the newspapers, and it seemed like he would show me new articles almost daily. He patiently answered every one of them, and finally the older masters opened their eyes and took pride in having contributed a major martial art to Japan.

HASSELL: It was about that time that Master Funakoshi opened his first dojo to the public. How did this come about?

NAKAYAMA: His first dojo was built about a year after I graduated from Takushoku University, and it was built through the efforts of his students. His most senior student was Kichinosuke Saigo, a famous political figure in Japan, and Mr. Saigo organized a committee to solicit donations for the construction of the dojo in 1938. This marked the building of the first karate dojo in Japan.

HASSELL: Was the dojo successful and well-received by the Japanese people in general?

NAKAYAMA: My feeling is that the development of Shotokan karate followed a special and very lucky developmental path. All of Master Funakoshi's early efforts were directed toward the teaching of the intelligentsia in Japan-doctors, lawyers, scholars, and artists. These people approached the art very seriously and from a high point of view. They studied hard and became very good, and they formed a very elite corps of senior students to represent Master Funakoshi's karate-do.

So, when the dojo opened to the public, the public in general had the feeling that the art was an art of virtuous and important people. These seniors did not teach the general public, and I think this served to set them apart in the public eye as a very special group of important karate people. By keeping them separate from the general public, Master Funakoshi was able to use them as a strong base-an important group of people in the public eye, thoroughly grounded in the basics and philosophy of his karate-do.

The general students who came in to train thus had a very high ideal to look up to, and we always encouraged them to emulate Master Funakoshi's older students. This really helped to set Shotokan karate-do apart from other styles in the public eye, and there is no doubt that it was a major contributing factor in the development of our large, international organization.

HASSELL: While we are on that subject, approximately how many members are there in the JKA worldwide today?

NAKAYAMA: It's difficult for me to say, because I head the technical side of the organization, and I'm not an administrator. I must confess that I don't keep a close eye on exact numbers.

But I would say that we have probably had about 10 million registered members since we started keeping careful records. Of course, it is hard to say how many of these members are actively training at any given moment. The number could be anywhere from two million to six million, and then there is the fact that we have many, many students practicing in colleges and universities, and the bulk of them would not be listed as regular JKA paying members. So, all I can tell you for sure is that the organization is active and healthy world-wide, and we have millions of members.

HASSELL: Sensei, you were obviously at the center of the most important period in the history of the development of karate in Japan. How does the overall system we use today compare with the system then in use, and how far away have we moved from Master Funakoshi's methods?

NAKAYAMA: During the years I was in college, Master Funakoshi developed and systematized Shotokan karate into three basic areas of training-kihon, which is basic training in fundamentals; kata, which is formal exercises; and kumite, which is sparring. He taught that these three areas are one and that they cannot be separated. But they are the theoretical basis for karate as an art, and they laid the foundation for us to research our techniques systematically and try to make them stronger.

Today, the JKA follows Master Funakoshi's method exactly. We do constantly research to try to find ways to make the body stronger and the techniques stronger, but we follow Master Funakoshi's methods exactly.

HASSELL: Has this research led to a lot of changes in techniques?

NAKAYAMA: We have not changed a single basic principle in all these years. What we have found through our research is that, by and large, Master Funakoshi's basic principles are correct, strong, and valid in the light of scientific evidence. When I say that there have been changes, I mean that with the advent of tournament competition, we have found it necessary to change the manner in which some techniques are applied for the specific application to competition. But basics are basics, and we have not changed them.

Some individuals have initiated changes, but their actions are wrong and unacceptable. Some people, for example, have gotten the mistaken notion that competition is everything, and they train with the sole purpose of winning the competition. This is absolutely wrong. Master Funakoshi's karate rests on the foundation of developing strong basic techniques first, through kihon and kata, and then using kumite to test the techniques against one another. Any other approach is not in keeping with his principles.

You see, before Master Funakoshi died, I began researching the idea of developing tournament, or sport karate. But when I asked Master Funakoshi for advice, he refused to comment. He was worried, you see, that if the tournament concept became too popular, then students would get away from the basic principles and practice only for tournament competition. He knew we would have karate tournaments and that they would be important for internationalizing karate, but he wanted it clearly understood that the most important thing would always be the basic training first.

That's why as long as I am Chief Instructor of the Japan Karate Association, the training will always be centered around Master Funakoshi's principles of kihon, kata and kumite. Strong basics first; tournament later.

HASSELL: Sensei, before we move on to some philosophical questions, could you tell us about your experiences in China, and how they influenced you in your karate training?

NAKAYAMA: Yes, I spent a great deal of time in China, and my experiences there strongly influenced my thinking about martial arts.

At Takushoku University, I was majoring in Chinese history and language (Mandarin), and I planned a trip to China in my sophomore year. The trip took on more significance for me because of an incident that occurred in the spring of my freshman year. I had been training in karate for several months by that time, and some friends and I went out to the country for a flower-viewing picnic. While we were minding our own business, some ruffians started giving us trouble, and I was very quick to show them the power of karate kicks and punches. I was very proud of being able to defend myself and my friends, but when Master Funakoshi heard about it, he was furious. He severely reprimanded me. He told me that I had good physical skills, but that I was emotionally and spiritually immature. He said that my actions were those of a coward and an immature child, and that true courage lies in self-restraint and self-discipline. It took much more courage, he said, to walk away when confronted with trouble than it did to just start punching and kicking everybody in sight.

His words had a profound effect on me, and I determined to make my trip to China a search for spiritual maturity. So, from June to September of my sophomore year, I traveled on foot through Manchuria, across the Greater Khingan Mountains, into Outer Mongolia. I practiced karate every day, but I was really lonely, afraid, and usually hungry. But in that vast solitude of Outer Mongolia, I think I began to grasp the essence of self-confidence and self-reliance. It helped me to see more clearly into my own nature, and I was able, for the most part, to overcome my loneliness and fear.

In 1937, I went to Peking as an exchange student to continue my study of Chinese language, society, and history. And wouldn't you know it! One of the first things I saw in China was Chinese boxing! At first, I wasn't very impressed with the Chinese arts as fighting methods. They emphasized circular movements, and they had no kime (focus) like Japanese karate, so I thought they were weak.

As time went by, though, I learned that the Chinese arts had a lot of value. The history of China is long and deep, and so is the history of her martial arts. I once saw an instructor receive a broken arm from what appeared to be a soft, circular block, and I decided that I must look deeper into the Chinese martial arts, so I began studying them, and continued studying them for almost ten years.

I trained very hard with many different instructors, and since I was also teaching karate, an art they had never seen, many of the instructors got to know me fairly well. In fact, when

a Japanese newspaper sent a film crew to do a story about Chinese martial arts, sifu (teachers) from all over China came to demonstrate for the cameras, and they asked me to act as their interpreter. As a courtesy to me, they also insisted that I demonstrate karate, so I did. In my demonstration, I emphasized kime and kata.

At this time, Japan and China were on the verge of war, and it was rather disconcerting to see the Japanese and Chinese newspapers squabbling over which country had the best martial arts. The Japanese said that Chinese boxing looked pretty, but lacked speed and kime, and was obviously no good for fighting. The Chinese retorted that while karate appeared to be fast and strong and extremely powerful, it was still just a brand-new martial art and lacked refinement and depth. Since I was teaching karate to a lot of sincere Chinese students and they were teaching me kung fu and tai chi, we found the whole affair amusing.

My own feeling was, and is, that while karate techniques rely on conservation of energy, which is released all at once at the end of a technique like an explosion, the Chinese arts waste a lot of energy in preparatory movements and deliver their power like the slow sweep of a sword.

But my training in China deeply impressed on me the idea that two cultures, so different on the outside, could both independently develop effective martial arts based on their individual cultures and rooted deeply in the same philosophical base-the philosophy of human beings seeking perfection of character through physical expression. That, to me, is the most important thing.

And please don't misunderstand; I'm not saying that Chinese martial arts are bad. I trained for a long time with an 80-year old sifu named Pai --- a famous Peking boxer --- who was absolutely extraordinary with his legs. He seemed to be able to wrap his leg around an attacking arm, and his defensive movements were marvelous. As a result of studying with him, I developed two new kicks that were incorporated into karate techniques by Master Funakoshi when I returned to Japan. One is a pushing kick or block using the sole of the foot or the lower portion of the leg, and the other is the reverse roundhouse kick.

HASSELL: How long did you remain in China?

NAKAYAMA: Until 1946. I spent 5 years at the university in Peking, and several more working for the Chinese government.

HASSELL: Conditions in Japan in 1946 weren't too good, were they?

NAKAYAMA: They were terrible! I had naively thought I could get a job teaching Chinese, but the whole country was immersed in reconstruction after the war, and there were very few academic jobs available. I worked as a dry goods salesman for a while to support myself.

One of the first things I did upon my return to Tokyo was to begin looking up my old comrades and karate seniors. But so many of them had been lost in the war!  Those who remained were not active in karate, for the most part. So I immediately moved to get us all together and start training again. I was fortunate, of course, because I had continued regular training during my years in China.

HASSELL: Wasn't it against the law to practice martial arts in Japan after the war?

NAKAYAMA: Yes, but the edict of the GHQ (General Headquarters of Allied Powers) was worded in such a way that it included karate as a part of judo. I had a friend who knew the head of the Education Bureau at the Ministry of Education, and he helped us convince the allied powers that karate was not part of judo at all. Using the premise that karate was actually a form of Chinese boxing-a sport-we received permission to practice. The GHQ thought karate was just a harmless pastime! So, while the other martial arts had to wait until the ban was lifted in 1948, we were able to practice and progress.

HASSELL: When was the JKA officially organized?

NAKAYAMA: We officially organized ourselves in May of 1949, and we were officially incorporated as an educational body under the Ministry of Education in 1955.

HASSELL: Sensei, in the United States, a lot of the karate in the 1950s was taught by returning GIs. How significant do you think their work was in introducing karate to America?

NAKAYAMA: The history of American karate really revolves around the decision of the Strategic Air Command (SAC) to teach martial arts to their personnel. In 1951, SAC sent 23 physical training instructors to the Kodokan in Tokyo to study the various martial arts under the leading instructors in Japan. This program continued for 15 years, and it exposed a large number of Americans to correct principles of karate, judo, aikido, and other martial arts.

Certainly the men who participated in this program had a significant impact on bringing karate to America.

But in retrospect, I think the biggest impact resulting from our association with the Americans was that we were forced to find ways to explain karate to non-Japanese people. It immediately became apparent to me and to Master Funakoshi that if we were going to teach Americans, we would have to provide a theoretical basis for our art. The Americans simply were not satisfied with blindly following like the Japanese.

So, under Master Funakoshi's guidance, I began an intense study of kinetics, physiology, anatomy and hygienics. We believed that with a thorough grounding in the scientific basis of body mechanics, we would find it easier to teach foreigners. We were right, and we also learned a great deal about our own practice of the art.

HASSELL: Did this study have any impact on the development of the *JKA Instructor Training Program*?

NAKAYAMA: Yes, indeed it did. When Master Funakoshi first brought karate to Japan, he was the only one qualified to teach. Later, when Master Kenwa Mabuni brought Shito-ryu karate to Osaka, the art began to spread rapidly, and there were many, many students.

This wide popularity led to the unfortunate situation in which individuals who had only six months of training under Master Funakoshi or Master Mabuni or someone else, started their own styles. By the time we organized the JKA and formed a corporation as an educational body under the Ministry of Education in 1955, there were about 200 so-called "styles" of karate around. And the public had no way of knowing who was qualified to teach and who was not. It was, therefore, our task to establish standards for instruction and to register these standards with the Ministry of Education.

So, under Master Funakoshi's guidance, I began formulating the Instructor Training Program. My feeling was that ranking should not be the only criteria for appointing instructors. It was even more important to teach them how to teach others. They needed broad knowledge of other areas like physics, anatomy, psychology, management, and so on. But this was a monumental task, and I had to have the help and advice of the more senior students. So, along with me, significant contributions were made to the program by Motokuni Sugiura, Teruyuki Okazaki, Hidetaka Nishiyama, and other senior instructors.

HASSELL: Sensei, many instructors in the West seem at a loss to explain the underlying philosophy of karate-do and martial arts in general to their students. I would like to ask you several philosophical questions and see if you can help us understand a little better.

NAKAYAMA: I'll try.

HASSELL: According to the majority of literature available in the West, it seems that karate-do shares a great deal with Zen and Buddhist philosophies, but very little with Shinto, which is the major Japanese religion. Is this impression correct, and if so, why?

NAKAYAMA: No, that impression is not correct. Martial arts in Japan, independent of Buddhism or Shinto, have a very long history, and the philosophy is deeply rooted in all aspects of Japanese life.

Karate is a martial way, like kendo and judo, and all these martial ways have their roots in the very beginning of Japanese culture. In the earliest wars, the instinct to live naturally brought out the concept of kill or die. That is, the warrior had to kill the enemy or be killed himself. This is very simple and natural.

From this, the Japanese warriors developed a philosophy, which is called heijo-shin kokoro michi, and this is the fundamental basis of all martial arts. What this means is that the warrior should strive to be the same on the outside no matter what he is doing or what he is facing. Whether he is simply going about his daily business or going to war and facing death, he must be the same and act the same-confident, calm and steadfast on the outside, and completely alert on the inside.

In those early times, the philosophies of Buddhism, Shinto and Confucianism were developing in Japan, and the martial artists studied these philosophies to gain a better grasp on how to effect heijo-shin kokoro michi-the calm and steadfast, "everyday" mind. Some of them studied Zen, and some studied Shintoism, but they were all studying from the same perspective. The choice of studying one religion or philosophy over another was simply that- a matter of personal choice. The backbone of their study was already there ---heijo-shin kokoro michi.

I know a lot of things are explained in the West in terms of one religion or philosophy or another, but if you look closely at Japanese culture, you will find, I believe, that heijo-shin kokoro michi, the philosophy of the warrior, permeates everything and is in fact the common denominator in the culture.

Noh and kabuki, for example, are based on the fundamental philosophy of budo. They require the abiding, clear, everyday mind, and there is no chance for a performer to correct a mistake. This is exactly the same as the philosophy of budo: There is only one chance to

execute the technique properly. Mistakes cannot be corrected. If you do it wrong, you die. This is especially true in kabuki.

Another factor that might make it seem that there is more influence on karate-do from Zen than Shinto is the fact that Zen Buddhism has specific physical forms and actions that must be used in meditation, but Shinto has no such outward, universal form. Shinto is based on the family and veneration of ancestors, and the form of rituals in Shinto follows no specific format. So, it logically follows that if one wants to explain one particular form, one will choose another philosophy or religion, like Zen Buddhism, for example, which has a readily discernible form, or format. How can one explain a formal system in terms of another system that has no form or format? So, perhaps it is natural that attempts to explain the philosophy of martial art center around Zen Buddhism more than around Shinto. But if students will study very carefully and especially study the principles of noh, kabuki and cha-no-yu (tea ceremony), they will come to understand that heijo-shin kokoro michi, the martial way philosophy, forms the basis of these arts, and that Zen Buddhism is not the basis of martial philosophy.

(continued on page 27)

PHOTOGRAPHS:

1 A young Sensei Nakayama posing after-party with some of the greatest karate masters of all time such as G. Yamaguchi, H. Othsuka and Manzo Iwata.

2 Gichin Funakoshi Sensei, the father of *Shoto Kan* karate and teacher of Sensei Nakayama.

3 Sensei Nakayama demonstrating a *shuto-uchi* against Sensei T. Okazaki.

4 Masatoshi Nakayama during his days in China.

5 Sensei Funakoshi's class. *(M. Nakayama shown at second right, kneeling)*.

6 *(inset)* Cover of the classic publication *Samurai* with Sensei T. Okazaki throwing a side kick as Sensei Nakayama performs *Soto Uke*.

PHOTOGRAPHS:

7 A young karate student posing for the camera.

8 Sensei Funakoshi with some advanced students including his son, Giko *(Sensei Nakayama pictured seated on the far right).*

9 Sensei Nakayama explaining *Jodan Uke* during one of his many seminars around the world.

10 Nakayama posing for the camera of German publisher Norbet Schiffer.

11 In company of some of the most relevant masters *(next to Gogen "The Cat" Yamaguchi)*

12 *(inset)* Sensei Kenwa Mabuni welcomes Sensei Funakoshi *(Sensei Obata and Sensei Nakayama shown in the background).*

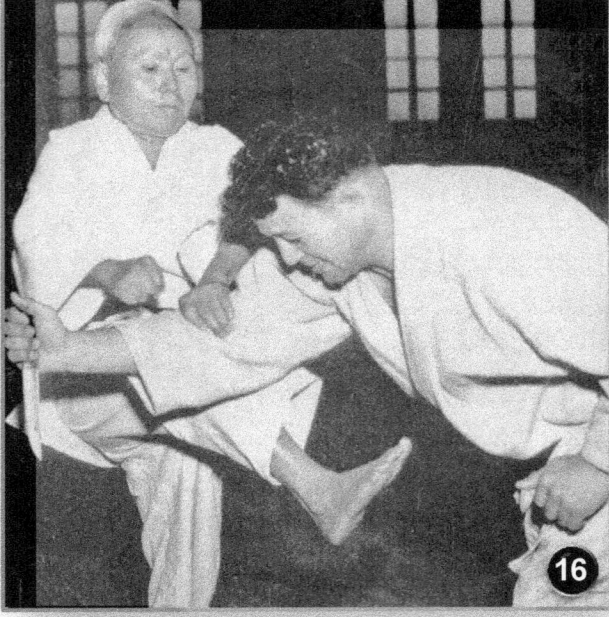

Photographs:

13 Sensei Nakayama posing in *Shuto Uke*.

14 With some of the best of that generation: Kanazawa Sensei and Okazaki Sensei.

15 In front of the J.K.A. Hombu Dojo.

16 Sensei Funakoshi applies a kicking technique on Mel Bruno.

17 Sensei Nakayama during a demonstration with Sensei Othsuka and Sensei Iwata.

PHOTOGRAPHS:

18 Explaining a technique, assisted by Sensei Koyama.

19 Author Sensei Randall Hassell interviewing Sensei Masatoshi Nayakayama.

20 In Tokyo, Japan --- Seiza with the best of Japanese Karate Association students.

21 Sensei Okazaki explains the biomechanics of the karate punch as Sensei Nakayama *(standing)* and Sensei Nishiyama listen.

22 *(inset)* The best J.K.A. instructors --- A generation of a lifetime.

PHOTOGRAPHS:

23 Posing with Sensei Asai in Hawaii.

24 Sensei Nakayama at his personal Dojo.

25 Receiving an award next to Sensei Othsuka.

26 During one of his many conversations with the acclaimed writer, Yukio Mishima.

PHOTOGRAPHS:

27 Sensei Teruyuki Okazaki, Sensei Gichin Funakoshi and Sensei Nakayama.

28 Reception in the U.S.A. by Sensei Nishiyama's group.

29 *(inset)* Sensei Nakayama leading a class at the original University Dojo in Tokyo.

Photographs:

30 Demonstrating a technique during a seminar in the U.S., assisted by Sensei Les Safar.

31 Relaxing pose with Sensei Funakoshi.

32 Leading a class during a private training session in the U.S.

33 Posing with students after a class at J.K.A. Honbu Dojo
(Sensei Nakayama seated at center)

Nakayama (continued from page 19)

HASSELL: Does *Yamato damashi* (the fighting spirit of Japan) relate in a significant way to karate-do, and if so, are Westerners capable of feeling it and understanding it? More simply, is it necessary for Westerners to understand Yamato damashi to understand karate-do?

NAKAYAMA: Yamato is the old name we used for Japan before we called it Nippon. Yamato damashi means "Japanese heart" (Nippon no kokoro) or "Japanese spirit," and every country has its own heart, its own particular spirit. One could therefore talk about America no damashi or America no kokoro.

The particular spirit or heart of Japan is centered around the samurai and their devotion to their lord, or daimyo. At the top of the structure is the Emperor, then comes the shogun, the daimyo, and the samurai. It is a lineal system in which the samurai gives over his entire being for the service of his lord, who in turn serves the shogun, who in turn serves the Emperor. The spirit of this system is one of self-sacrifice and self-denial on the part of the samurai, first for the good of his daimyo, and ultimately for the good of his Emperor and the country.

The spirit of America would be a bit different, but would manifest itself in the same way in times of crisis. During a war, for example, the American people practice self-sacrifice and self-denial for the good of their country at large. And they have an intense spirit that binds them together and enables them to defeat any enemy.

Every country has its own version of this spirit, and people in every country will die for the benefit of the general good. It is a matter of loyalty and love of country. However, each society is different, and each has its own version of loyalty and pride. Some sacrifice for their lord, some for their president, some for their prime minister, and so on.

In the sense that Yamato damashi refers specifically to the spirit of Japan, it is not necessary for non-Japanese to understand and feel it to understand and feel the essence of budo. Budo no kokoro, the spirit of budo, is essentially the same as Yamato damashi, but this heart and spirit is not limited to the specific spirit of Japan. Rather, it is a universal spirit that will be interpreted and reinforced by people in various cultures according to their own cultural history and needs.

So, if people study the principles of budo-the deeper, philosophical principles-they will gain the spirit of budo according to the spirit of their own country.

In other words, I see no reason to relate budo to Yamato damashi specifically. A person who is training in the budo spirit of self-sacrifice and self-denial will derive great understanding and benefits, centering around his own culture and his own country.

The development of heart or spirit is a natural outgrowth of budo training.

HASSELL: How do the fighting strategies of sen-no-sen and go-no-sen relate to Master Funakoshi's famous principle of karate ni sente nashi (there is no first attack in karate)?

NAKAYAMA: In my books, Best Karate, volumes three and four, I used Mr. Iida's techniques as a good example of go-no-sen, and Mr. Oishi's techniques as a prime example of sen-no-sen. And that is exactly what these terms refer to-techniques of fighting. Karate ni sente nashi, on the other hand, has nothing to do with technique. Rather, it is a statement relating to personal spirit or sense of being. It is an admonition to control yourself and not fight.

"Karate ni sente nashi" means literally that there is no first attack in karate. But this does not simply mean that the karateka will not make the initial move to start a fight. Master Funakoshi repeatedly told us that it is also a strict prohibition against carelessly using the techniques of karate. This spirit is embodied in the kata, each of which begins with a defensive movement. This also means that a karateka should never act in a manner that could create an atmosphere of trouble, and he should avoid places where trouble is likely to occur. If a student frequents a bar where fights occur on a regular basis and he is suddenly called upon to use his techniques in self-defense, then he does not understand the meaning of karate ni sente nashi. In effect, he started the fight because he knew trouble was likely, and he could have avoided the conflict altogether by simply not going there.

Karate ni sente nashi is a wish for harmony among people. In the kata, "Kanku Dai", this wish for harmony is symbolized in the first movement, which is unlike any other kata and which does not relate directly to defense and attack. The hands are raised together above the head, palms outward, and the karateka looks at the sky through the hole formed by his fingers and thumbs. This movement expresses identification with nature, tranquility of mind and body, and the wish for harmony. The karateka who understands this will have a modest heart, a gentle attitude, and a wish for harmony.

On the technical side, go-no-sen means the attack is coming, you can see it, and you will attempt to counter-attack. Sen-no-sen means that you don't give the opponent a chance; you overwhelm him with continuous attack.

But these terms refer to the psychological states inherent in fighting situations. For example, when a cat stalks and kills a mouse, the cat is, in effect, practicing sen-no-sen. He gives the mouse no chance at all. But sen-no-sen does not refer to a specific technique. It just refers to the fact that the cat is not giving the mouse a chance at all. Go-no-sen would have no meaning for the cat unless he were being attacked by a 100-pound dog.

I use this analogy to point out the fact that neither strategy is superior to the other. The strategy employed depends on the situation and the psychological make-up of the individual. If one person is exceptionally skilled at sen-no-sen, and his opponent is exceptionally skilled at go-no-sen, it is impossible to say which is going to win. The strategies are of equal importance and effectiveness, depending on the individual and the circumstances.

Another important saying in karate-do, in addition to "There is no first attack in karate," is "There is no posture (kamae) in karate." This latter saying applies directly to the attitude necessary in training or actual fighting. What it means is that the student must not stiffen the body and make it rigid; one should always be relaxed and alert.

In Japan, we say that one should be flexible like bamboo, which bends and snaps back when the wind blows; one who is stiff will break in the wind like the rigid oak tree.

On the other hand, relaxation does not mean lack of alertness. Sometimes I tell students that there is posture, but no posture. What I mean is that there is mental posture, but no physical posture. At the very highest levels of development, though, the karate-ka should have no posture at all-not posture of mind, and not posture of body.

This is very difficult to grasp, but it is essential to grasp it in order to master karate-do. This concept was summarized in the 17th century by the Zen priest, Takuan, in his famous letter to the swordsman, Yagyu Munenori. What Takuan told Yagyu, essentially, is that if you place your mind on the movements of your opponent, your mind will be filled with the movements of your opponent. Likewise, if the mind is fixed on the opponent's sword, or on your own sword, or on the cutting of the opponent, or on the fear of being cut yourself, it will be totally

absorbed by whatever it is fixed on, and defeat will be inevitable.

Takuan's solution to the problem was to suggest that the mind be placed nowhere --- that it be spread out throughout the entire body, concentrating on nothing in particular. That way, he said, the mind will serve whatever part of the situation needs immediate attention. If the arms need to move, the mind will move them; if the legs need to move, the mind will move them.

What he is saying, in effect, is that if the mind is placed nowhere, it will be everywhere.

This philosophy arises directly from Zen's desire to have no attachments to anything. The "kara" of karate comes from Mahayana Buddhism, and is also pronounced ku, which, translated into English, means "void" or "nothingness." Its original meaning was "to be lacking in" or "to be wanting in," and it calls for the individual to escape from the rules and differences between good and bad, reality and illusion. This, according to Mahayana Buddhism, strengthens the individual's ethics in that if one is attached to nothing, one will naturally choose good over evil.

I know this is difficult, but the essence of it is to let the mind go, and to act naturally. When a person first sits behind the wheel of a car, for example, a lot of attention must be given to details: 'This is the accelerator; this is the brake. This makes it go, this makes it stop," and so on.

After a while, however, we don't have to think about these things on a conscious level. We just get in the car and go, and when we need to stop, we naturally put a foot on the brake pedal.

This is the same process we use in karate-do. When we begin training, we have no posture of mind or technique. If we are attacked, we respond naturally, and flail away at the opponent. As we study posture and technique, we devise strategies and movements, and we learn a plan for defending ourselves and counter-attacking. But this takes away our natural spontaneity, and our minds are fixed on specific postures, techniques, and strategies. After many, many years of training, we return to our natural state-transcending techniques and postures and strategies-and we again respond without thought. Of course, after many years of training, we are able to respond much more efficiently and effectively.

The time required to attain the spontaneous mind, which is at once nowhere and everywhere, is a lifetime, no matter how long one lives.

HASSELL: How, then, does karate's go-no-sen differ from the bujutsu concept of satsui-o-kanjiru?

NAKAYAMA: *Satsui-o-kanjiru literally means "to be in a killing mood," and it refers to a situation in which one samurai would be hiding, waiting for an enemy to walk by. But it is not simply a matter of waiting for the enemy to appear; it is more a matter of sensing when the opponent is near, and killing him before a fight can occur. It implies that the one in hiding cannot see the enemy, but can sense or feel when the enemy is near and kill him instantly before a fight starts. If the samurai who is walking by is practicing go-no-sen, he must also feel or sense when the attack is coming and defend himself.*

HASSELL: The famous martial artist, Yamada Jirokichi, a kendo master, has said that modern budo disciplines like karate-do and judo are producing experts with a very narrow, limited range of skills. He says they train only with one weapon or only in empty-hand techniques, like in karate-do, and that modern-day experts are not up to par with the experts of old. If this is true, why doesn't Shotokan karate-do teach its students the use of traditional weapons to broaden their base of skills?

NAKAYAMA: *I think this criticism misses the purpose of budo training as opposed to the purpose of bujutsu training. The study of bujutsu in feudal times encouraged the warrior to become as proficient as possible in as wide an array of weapons as possible. This was a* practical approach for warriors who were actually fighting on the battlefield and facing enemies on a regular basis. But the purpose of budo is not to gain a wide knowledge for the purpose of fighting; rather, the purpose of budo is to gain a very, very deep knowledge of one's art in order to perfect one's character and see more clearly and deeply into the nature of one's existence.

Master Funakoshi, of course, studied many weapons like the sai, bo, and nunchaku in Okinawa, but when he moved karate-jutsu in the direction of karate-do, he followed the example of other forms of budo. That is, he examined the existing weapons and techniques, and he chose those techniques that were fundamental to his system of budo and which, if studied very deeply and intensely, would lead the student to a deep understanding of efficient body motion, self-defense, and so on.

If the purpose of budo is to go more deeply into life, then this approach makes sense. If you think about it logically, there is simply not enough time in one lifetime to master a wide array of weapons or systems or different arts. It is possible to have a good working knowledge of many different things, but it is not possible to master all of them. We concentrate on the techniques of karate-do and try to truly master them.

This is similar to the way medicine is taught to doctors today. A doctor can be a general practitioner with very good skills, but he cannot be a master of everything. He cannot specialize in every aspect of medicine. Those who want to specialize get their basics first, and then they spend more years in school intensely studying one particular field like orthopedics, ophthalmology, or cardiology. They become specialists in their field, and they have vastly more knowledge about their field than does the average doctor.

In budo, the idea is the same. We want to have a broad, basic foundation of knowledge about body motion and self-defense, and then we specialize to become expert in a particular art.

Your question is a very important one, and it is important that people understand the difference between bujutsu and budo.

In pre-Tokugawa Japan, the bujutsu arts were studied widely by the samurai. Then, at the time of Tokugawa, the arts were separated into distinct, individual arts, like the sword, spear, and ninjutsu, with the purpose of going more deeply into these arts for the seeking of character perfection, and to individually study the arts and raise them to very high levels of development.

The same thing happened in Okinawa, where the early masters of Chinese hand (tode) studied everything from punching and kicking to knife throwing. Then they separated the arts, and some studied one while others specialized in another.

Another important point is that the fundamental ideas of almost all the budo forms are the same. That is, Master Funakoshi had studied the weaponry, and I did, too, for that matter, and the movements and techniques of Shotokan karate-do are based on approximately the same fundamental movements as the weapons: bo, sai, spear, and the like.

So, if one studies and masters the techniques of karate-do, he will be able to rather easily pick up the techniques of these weapons. And I want to emphasize that there is nothing wrong with practicing and having a working knowledge of these weapons or even other martial arts, but it is essential to never lose sight of the purpose of budo training.

It is better, I feel, to concentrate on trying to master one art completely, and this takes a lifetime of consistent, hard work.

HASSELL: We know that in Shotokan karate there are 15 basic kata-five Heian, three Tekki, Bassai Dai, Kanku Dai, Jion, Jutte, Empi, Hangetsu, and Gankaku -- but JKA students practice a number of other kata, also. And in other schools of Shotokan, some of the students practice Taikyoku and Ten-no-kata. Can you tell us where these other kata came from and why we are encouraged to practice them?

NAKAYAMA: The precise origins of many of the kata are lost in the mists of history. However, to take one example, the kata we now call Kanku Dai was formerly called Kushanku and we practice it exactly the way Master Funakoshi interpreted it. But it derives from a form originally called Koshukon, and it is believed that this kata was taught to many Okinawans by a Chinese attaché. Many, many people learned this kata and then went their separate ways, developing and studying their own arts. Over time, they changed the basic form of the kata to suit the needs of their particular style or particular body structure or particular needs. Consequently, there were, and are now, many different forms of the kata, Koshukon.

The same is true of Bassai Dai. There are even more versions of Bassai than there are of Koshukon. The famous master, Matsumura, was noted for his practice and development of Bassai, and many people learned the kata from him. Again, these individuals in many cases changed the kata to suit their own needs, and today the number of different versions of Bassai is probably in the hundreds. But Master Funakoshi chose the form of the kata that he felt was the most effective, and we practice that form of the kata. So, the kata we call Kanku

Sho and Bassai Sho are simply well-known variations of the original kata, Kanku and Bassai.

The way they came to be practiced among Master Funakoshi's students is not really a matter of deeper meaning or significance. It is a matter of human nature. Some of the older students, chief among them being Master Funakoshi's son, Yoshitaka, would, from time to time, practice some of these versions they had learned elsewhere, and the younger students would be fascinated. We would imitate our seniors and ask them to teach us these different forms. They would teach us, but then they would always say, "There is nothing wrong with practicing another form, but remember that you must always concentrate on mastering the 15 basic forms. They are all you need to fully master karate, and you must not neglect them."

A kata that was developed and introduced by Yoshitaka Sensei, for example, is Sochin. Sochin was his specialty, and we learned it from him, but it is not one of the essential 15 kata.

Master Funakoshi probably considered our desire to learn these other kata as youthful exuberance, but there was no harm in picking up different ideas from different kata. It is useful, but not, according to Master Funakoshi, essential.

Some of the kata have come into the JKA system because Master Funakoshi took me around Japan to visit and pay courtesy calls on some of the other old masters in Osaka, Kyoto,

Okuyama, and Hiroshima. We would exchange ideas with these masters, and they were, of course, anxious to learn Master Funakoshi's kata.

In one instance, I remember we visited the founder of Shito-ryu karate-do, Kenwa Mabuni. Well, Master Funakoshi had already studied the Goju and Shito styles of karate and had incorporated the basic elements of these styles into Shotokan. The kata, Hangetsu, for example, is essentially a Goju-style kata.

If one practices Hangetsu, it is very easy to then exercise the Goju kata Tensho and Sanchin. Gankaku and Empi, on the other hand are essentially Shorin-style kata.

But Master Funakoshi never ceased his study of other forms of karate, and when we visited Master Mabuni, Master Funakoshi told me to learn Gojushiho and Nijushiho so we could study them more carefully. So Kenwa Mabuni taught me these kata.

Just as a natural outgrowth of our study of these kata, the kata eventually changed their form to conform to the form of movement of Shotokan karate, and they are now practiced by many of our members.

But the most important thing I want to say about all of this is that I consider myself to be one of the luckiest human beings alive. I was so lucky to train under Master Funakoshi!

His genius lay in his deep wisdom and judgment. He literally created Shotokan karate from the elements of all the different styles of karate in existence. Shotokan contains elements of both Goju-ryu and Shito-ryu, and if a person devotes himself to the mastery of Master Funakoshi's 15 kata, he will be able to easily pick up the essence of any other style of karate.

Master Funakoshi was looking to the future when he created Shotokan-looking toward the day when all of karate would be united into one-and we will always be indebted to him for his work.

HASSELL: Sensei, you say that Master Funakoshi taught the students Heian, Tekki, then Bassai and Kanku, and then moved on to the other kata?

NAKAYAMA: Yes. The first kata learned was always Heian Shodan.

HASSELL: Could you explain, then, where the kata practiced by some other schools of Shotokan - Taikyoku-no-kata and Ten-no-kata came from?

NAKAYAMA: Master Funakoshi never taught us those forms. They were created as basic training methods by Yoshitaka Funakoshi and Genshin Hironishi, but they were never taught or practiced by Master Funakoshi. The principles of these forms do not conform to the principles of kata. They are not kata; they are basic training methods. But they were never taught by Master Funakoshi.

Master Minoru Miyata was asked by Yoshitaka Sensei and Genshin Hironishi to pose for photographs to illustrate the movements of Taikyoku and Ten-no-kata, and out of respect for Yoshitaka, the Master's son, he consented. But even though the photos of Mr. Miyata were used to introduce these forms, he, himself, never learned them or practiced them. In Japan, the only group that knows these forms is the Waseda University group. Even Keio University, the oldest of the Shotokan clubs, has no knowledge of them.

The purpose of the forms was to provide a basic training method to be used before the students learned Heian kata. But both before and after my trip to China, I trained with Master Funakoshi virtually every day, and he never once mentioned Taikyoku or Ten-no-kata. Not even once.

If this is a matter of concern, I would point to the Master's official text, Karate-do Kyohan. If he wanted us to know these forms, why didn't he put them in Karate-do Kyohan?

HASSELL: Sensei those forms do appear in the English version of Karate-do Kyohan.

NAKAYAMA: *Really? I haven't read the English version, but I can tell you that they positively are not in the original Japanese version.*

HASSELL: Sensei, so much of the last 20 years has been devoted to the development of sport karate that today there are tournaments everywhere, virtually all the time. Does the future of karate-do, in your opinion, revolve around the concept of sport karate and its continued development?

NAKAYAMA: *Karate has reached its present high level of development because its practitioners have followed exactly the principles of Master Funakoshi. The most important thing has been, and will continue to be, the practice of strong, fundamental karate for the purpose of physical education, self-defense, and spiritual discipline. Karate training is for the development of the individual-emotionally, physically, and spiritually.*

The karate tournament exists to spread karate more widely to the general public. Sport is a good way to do this. It proves to the public that we are not a bunch of vicious killers, and it shows them that anyone can participate in karate, and, if they so desire, compete safely.

If we ever center the development of karate around sport, we will lose our essence as a martial art, and obviously, I don't want this to happen. I want karate to continue to develop along the same lines and by the same methods we have had in the past.

Before students compete, they should work hard and consistently to gain a strong foundation in the basics and a thorough understanding of karate's spiritual principles.

In my day, you see, we had no tournaments or competition of any kind with others. Our only competition was with ourselves, and this is the way it should be. We never trained to get a point in a tournament. Our main training device was the makiwara, and we spent hours and hours learning how to use it. We would begin by hitting it a few times and gradually building up to the point where it could be struck as many as a thousand times without pain or injury. We would often warm up for class by punching the makiwara 500 or 1,000 times. Our only interest in those days was developing strong techniques, and I believe this is as it should be.

Sparring will teach the student timing and distancing, but there is nothing like the makiwara to develop a strong body and strong will. I encourage every student to forge his own muscles and will on the makiwara every day.

HASSELL: With that philosophy as a base, how, then, did sport karate come to occupy such an important place in modern karate?

NAKAYAMA: As I indicated earlier, in my early training I and a lot of other young students wanted some form of combat because of our previous training in kendo and judo. We just weren't satisfied with kata all the time. Even though he was reluctant, Master Funakoshi gradually began introducing us to five-step, one-step, and finally free sparring. I don't think he especially liked doing this, because he was very adamant on the point that karate was not a barbarous, combative art. On the other hand, he realized that the younger generation would have to have something more, and he also wanted karate to occupy an equal position with judo and kendo.

By 1935, various college clubs all over Japan were staging what they called "kokangeiko" (exchange of courtesies and practice). These exchanges were supposed to consist of kata practice and one-step sparring with prearranged attacks and defenses. In reality, they often degenerated into brawls. I saw broken noses and jaws, teeth knocked out and ears almost ripped off.

I was torn between the belief that karate needed a combative aspect and the sure knowledge that someone was going to be killed if this sort of thing went unchecked. Especially in the pacifistic atmosphere of post-war Japan, I saw kendo and judo flourishing as sports, and I was concerned that if karate continued on its bloody course, the people would reject it.

My solution was to study the rules of many different kinds of sports, and to experiment with various ideas of competition. Once, for example, I set up matches in which contestants wore heavy padding and fought full-contact. The padding was designed on the order of kendo armor, but it was, of course, much lighter. To my great dismay, we found that the armor itself, because of its bulkiness and restriction of movement, caused more injuries than it prevented. Finally, the committee members and I came up with what we thought would be a viable set of rules for sparring.

These rules were used in the first All Japan Karate Championship Tournament in Tokyo in 1957, and the tournament was very successful. Prior to 1953, there were no organized public tournaments in Japan, or anywhere else, for that matter. In effect, our tournament in 1957 was the first world karate championship.

My greatest concern at that time was to insure that karate, if given a sporting aspect, would not lose its essence as an art. I therefore worked very hard on designing kata competition, and I based the rules on the rules of skating and gymnastics competitions.

My one hope was to preserve the essence of karate-do as an art of self-defense and self-denial, and to prevent the excitement of sparring from transforming karate into a mere sport.

HASSELL: What, then, is your opinion of modern, full-contact karate?

NAKAYAMA: The full-contact karate in America and Europe certainly has a place in the world of karate, but it is not karate-do. Do means "way" or "path," and it means that the art is a vehicle for improving human character. What is most important to understand is that this seeking after better character is not a temporary or fleeting goal. It is a life-long process that must be pursued every day through training.

Sport develops the contestants in a straight line. That is, they train hard in the physical techniques until they become strong, and then they compete. As they compete, they become stronger and stronger, and some become champions. But after a certain number of years, the body begins to decline, and the contestant can no longer compete effectively. One progresses steadily toward a narrow ideal, which is reached at the peak of youth, and then age brings a straight decline.

Karate-do, on the other hand, has no such narrow ideal as the winning of championships, and human progress in the art is like climbing a series of stairs or steep steps. As the mind and body grow together, the student moves continuously onward and upward, one step at a time. Even when the body declines, there is still another step ahead in the seeking of character perfection. Until the day you die, the process is endless, because no one is perfect, but we can all become a little better if we keep trying.

Full-contact karate is like boxing in that it is all based on force—the strongest person wins. While there is nothing wrong with that, and certainly nothing wrong with making contact, it is very important, I believe, to develop the human spirit through controlled techniques. This is one of the pillars of karate-do competition. In order to execute a fast, powerful technique and to stop it with perfect control and precision, requires total control of the mind.

In sport, the emphasis is on the strong body; in karate-do the emphasis is on the mind. Everything begins and ends with the mind, and this gives the karate-ka qualities that he can carry over into his daily life and use to his benefit.

This control also enables the karate-ka to control his blows with whatever force is necessary. In a self-defense situation, the thoroughly trained karate-ka will always find the right distance, and the correct amount of force will be delivered to the target.

HASSELL: That said, should karate be in the Olympics?

NAKAYAMA: *I am not opposed to karate being in the Olympics, but I have grave concerns about the consequences of it. Consider what happened to judo when it became an Olympic sport. Rather than retain its foundation as a martial way, judo was changed to fit the structure of the Olympics. The Kodokan lost control of the art, and the students started training primarily to gain the competitive "edge" which would enable them to compete in the Olympics. This has had a devastating effect on judo in Japan, and the judo leaders there are now in a period of excruciating self-examination. They face a real dilemma in trying to return judo to its origins as a martial way that can be practiced by anyone-young or old, man, woman, or child. The sport aspect has become the over-riding concern of most judoka, and this is not in keeping with Jigoro Kano's (the founder of judo) principles.*

So, I believe that if karate gets into the Olympics, it will be okay provided that karate does not lose its essence as a martial way-a way of life that can be practiced by anyone. If that can happen, everything will be all right. But I have grave concerns about this, and I certainly do not think that gaining Olympic recognition should be our primary goal.

HASSELL: Sensei, even in the JKA today, we see competitors wearing protective padding on their hands. Isn't this getting pretty far away from the original concept of karate as a martial art and changing the art to conform to the sport?

NAKAYAMA: *Actually, I think this may help to more clearly delineate the difference between sport karate and basic, fundamental karate. Realistically, if we are going to have sport matches, then we should do everything possible to make them safe. And there is little doubt that sport karate is going to grow in the future, and will probably one day become an Olympic sport. When that happens, we should be prepared to show the Olympic Committee that we have safeguards against injury. Light hand pads are a step in that direction, and I don't think they will significantly change the face of karate as a martial art. They are simply a practical safety device for sport competition. They are not in general use in the JKA, by the way, except in team matches in selected tournaments.*

HASSELL: What is your hope for karate 10 years from now?

NAKAYAMA: I hope that 10 years from now, people will understand that karate is a martial way and that they will still be practicing real, basic karate as physical education, as self-defense, and as a method of spiritual development. Particularly in the area of sport, I hope the contestants will not train simply to gain a point. I hope they will remember the basis of karate as a way of life and will train in the basics and try to effect "ikken hisatsu" - to stop the opponent with one blow. I hope they will practice to make one strong punch and one strong kick. If they continue to train in this way, they will be able to control their techniques. If they practice simply to score a point, however, they will never be able to control their techniques or themselves. This kind of training leads to many injuries.

Karate in the future should be as it has been in the past. That is, students who train seriously under a good instructor should first gain good health from the physical exercise. This training will lead to strong basic techniques and good self-defense skills. After these two factors have been obtained, then there is nothing wrong with competing to test each other-technique against technique, spirit against spirit. Training in this fashion leads to a good competition or tournament in which the contestants display real, true karate.

So, when I say that karate has three main aspects, I mean that it is applicable as physical education, as self-defense, and as a new style of martial art-sport. Underlying all of these aspects is the fundamental basis of karate serving the individual for spiritual development.

All modern martial arts, like judo, for example, are this way, also. Originally, when the techniques of karate were first developing, the rationale was very simple: we face each other, and either you kill me or I am going to kill you. These arts were born in eras of war. In modern times, however, we aren't facing the same situations as those who first used the arts for self-protection. The development of budo as opposed to bujutsu rests on the foundation of developing spiritual strength and strength of character. This is the main value of budo for human beings. The most important thing for future generations to keep in mind is that karate serves to develop a philosophy, an ethical way of life. If this is developed first in the contestants, there will be no problem with sport competition. We simply must keep in mind our fundamental purposes.

HASSELL: Virtually all of the JKA instructors in the West, both Japanese and American, say the same things you are saying about the importance of studying karate-do as a way of life and spiritual development, but it is sometimes difficult to perceive this deeper development going on in the dojo. In other words, we talk about spiritual development, but seem to place an awful lot of emphasis on sport. Twenty years ago, for example, there was very little emphasis on free sparring for competition, and a lot of emphasis on one-step and semi-free, one-step sparring. Do you think we are moving in the right direction at this moment, or are we getting too far away from the ideals of karate training as you perceive them?

NAKAYAMA: I think this is a very, very difficult time for karate-do and those who are trying to teach it correctly. We are at a pivotal point in the history of the development of the art and, by and large, I think things are progressing in a correct manner.

What must be understood is that, from a historical viewpoint, it wasn't so many years ago that karate was practiced only in complete secrecy. I don't think that was any better for the art than training solely for competition would be. The point is that times change, circumstances change, and people adjust themselves and their arts to the times and the circumstances.

What we need, I believe, is a balance in everything we do. Sport karate is a new innovation, and it will take some more time before we can assimilate it completely and adjust ourselves to it.

I think the instructors in the JKA, both in Japan and in America, are doing a very good job of studying the sport aspect of the art and are transmitting it in a proper fashion. What is needed is time. In time, as long as we remain committed to the fundamental principles of Master Funakoshi, we will find the proper balance between sport competition and basic training.

HASSELL: The majority of instructors would certainly agree that this is a difficult time for teaching karate-do. What specific advice would you give them to help them accomplish their task efficiently?

NAKAYAMA: I would tell them, no matter what, to keep training diligently in their art and to keep their mind focused on Master Funakoshi's principles of karate-do as a way of life. If they do this, they will succeed. Frankly, as long as the instructors proceed in this fashion, I will have no worries about the future of karate-do.

HASSELL: You say that times are changing, and that we must seek a balance between all aspects of the art. Does this mean, then, that instructors should teach the fundamental precepts of kumite like "ikken hisatsu" (to finish the opponent with one blow) separately from kumite for competition? In other words, is there a difference between sparring in the dojo in daily training and sparring in competition?

NAKAYAMA: No, absolutely not. In the sense of heijo-shin kokoro michi, which I explained earlier, the karate-ka must train daily and be prepared at all times to do whatever is necessary. He must be calm and steadfast, whether he is training in the dojo, eating breakfast, or competing in a shiai. If we train seriously in the dojo, learning and applying the basic principles, we will then be ready for anything that happens, at any time.

Correct training in karate's underlying principles will enable the karate-ka to walk out of the dojo and defend himself if necessary, or walk out of the dojo and compete in a shiai. If the basic principles are correct, it will make no difference what the karate-ka is doing.

The basics are the basics, and they will serve the karate-ka well at all times, under any circumstances.

I know it's difficult to comprehend, and even more difficult to teach, but there must be no separation of technique into categories of self-defense, sport, and so on. Consider that technique is technique, and if the karate-ka is training properly, he will be able to use his

training to defend himself and to compete. If a student is trained only for competition, for example, and he is mugged while walking to the auditorium for a tournament, he will be in perilous straits. Wouldn't that be ridiculous—a tournament champion who couldn't defend himself in a real situation!

Karate-do serves to develop the whole individual, and it is the individual who must respond to any situation as it arises. If he can only respond in a tournament, there is something drastically wrong with his training.

HASSELL: What do you think of those who train in different systems at the same time?

NAKAYAMA: Everybody can do what they please, and I respect any position. For me, as a budoka, the idea of budo is to train, study, and develop one art so using this as a vehicle we'll improve as human beings. The important aspect is not to learn more and more systems but to go deep into one art so you can develop the correct spirit of budo, which goes deeply into life. If you use logic, in a lifetime it is impossible to develop true mastery in many styles and methods; maybe you'll reach a level of simple physical skill but not true mastery. The correct idea of budo is to concentrate on something and master it. I always compare this to a doctor. There are many branches of medicine but doctors become specialist in their fields. They know more than any other average doctor in that specific field. In short, the idea is to go deep into one art since after many years of training you'll be able to understand any other system and grasp the essence of it. Once again, I want to emphasize that this is the budo attitude and approach.

HASSELL: Any fear or regrets after all these years?

NAKAYAMA: No, not really – no regrets. Maybe a few things could have been done in a different way but I always tried my best to promote and expand the art of karate-do all over the world. And fears? I hope when I die and meet Sensei Funakoshi that he's not angry with me for introducing the sportive aspect into the art. After all, he wanted to see his art practiced and recognized all around the world and the sportive aspects did just that.

HASSELL: Finally, Sensei, if you were permitted time to say only one thing to the people who are training in JKA karate today, both students and instructors, what would you say to them?

NAKAYAMA: I would tell them to meditate on the words of Anton Geesink, the Dutchman who defeated the Japanese and won the World Judo Championship. Geesink faced and defeated every major Japanese judo competitor, and he shook the very foundations of martial arts in Japan. It was just unthinkable that a young European could so skillfully and cleanly destroy the Japanese masters in their own art. But that is exactly what he did.

I remember that the leaders of judo and even some other martial arts in Japan were in a tremendous uproar, and they made elaborate and detailed plans to study Geesink's "secrets" of competition. Ultimately, they arranged for a Japanese journalist to interview Geesink in depth to try to discover the training methods this man had used to defeat the Japanese.

Geesink's answer was perhaps the most important statement I have heard in all my years in karate-do, and I will never forget it. He said:

The Japanese have devoted themselves to the study of judo for competition. They have gone to extraordinary lengths to develop winning contestants and fine champions. I, on the other hand, have never trained for competition in my life. All I have ever done is trained in judo as a way of life, exactly as Dr. Kano taught. While the Japanese were devising competitive strategies, I was in the dojo, practicing basics and kata.

I defeated the Japanese because I know judo better than the Japanese. The 'secret' is to train every day in the basics. This will make you unbeatable.

*The meaning of karate-do goes beyond victory
in a contest of mastery or self-defense techniques.
Unlike common sports, karate-do has a
soul of its own. To be a true master is to understand
the soul of karate-do as a martial Way.
Karate-do has grown popular these days, and its
soul is apt to pass from our minds.*

--- Sensei Nakayama

www.ingramcontent.com/pod-product-compliance
Lightning Source LLC
Chambersburg PA
CBHW080528110426
42742CB00017B/3273